Table of Contents

Laboratory Exercises in Biology

Dr. J. Christopher Gaiser
Dr. Sreerupa Ray
Dr. Catherine Reinke
Dr. Jeremy Weisz

Biology 210
Fall 2023
Principles of Biology
Linfield College
Department of Biology

Microscope Calibration

Power (ocular x objective)	Value of each ocular micrometer unit (mm)	Approximate field of view (diameter in mm)
40X	0.03	4.0
100X	0.01	1.9
400X	0.003	0.40
1000X	0.001	0.19

Drawings

Drawings should include the following:
- Title
- Power (ocular x objective)
- Actual size (measured using the ocular micrometer)
- Magnification (drawing size / actual size)

Fall 2023 Laboratory Schedule

WEEK OF:	EXERCISE
Aug 28	Osmosis & Diffusion I / Assessment Exam
Sep 4	Osmosis & Diffusion II / Tiny Earth (TE) – Introduction
Sep 11	Enzymes
Sep 18	TE – Isolate soil bacteria and dilution plating
Sep 25	TE – Calculate CFU per gram and create master plates
Oct 2	Photosynthesis
Oct 9	**Fall Break** – Special lab schedule
Oct 16	TE – Run inhibition experiments
Oct 23	TE – Identify antibiotic producers, streak to isolate / ESKAPE presentations
Oct 30	TE – Re-streak isolates / Mitosis
Nov 6	TE – PCR of selected isolates / Gram staining of isolates
Nov 13	*Drosophila* – Set up cross
Nov 20	**NO LAB – Thanksgiving**
Nov 27	*Drosophila* – Begin scoring / Meiosis
Dec 4	*Drosophila* – Finish scoring / TE Presentations

Laboratory Grading, Protocols, and Safety Procedures

GRADING

Lab is worth 200 points (one-third of your total grade) and includes completing worksheets, laboratory reports, group presentations, a laboratory notebook, and additional assignments. Late lab assignments will be graded down 20% for each day late.

LABORATORY PROTOCOLS

1. <u>Attendance</u> - Laboratory attendance is mandatory. If, for a compelling reason, you need to attend a different section, make arrangements with Ken Kebisek, *in advance*. Laboratory make-ups are provided for excused absences only and *must be completed in the same week*.

    NOTE: Having two or more unexcused lab absences and/or missing lab assignments will result in failure of the laboratory component of the course (receive a zero).

2. <u>Punctuality</u> – Lab sections begin promptly at 1:00 PM. You are expected to be on time.

3. <u>Pre-Lab Assignments</u> - Prior to a lab, you may be required to submit a pre-lab assignment. Information regarding these assignments will be given in lab every week.

4. <u>Preparation</u> - You are expected to come to lab prepared. You should have read and studied the current week's lab exercise and completed any pre-lab assigned. All assignments are due at the start of a lab period. Please do not delay or disrupt the start of lab turning in assignments. Wait until an appropriate, later time to do so.

5. <u>Smart Phones</u> – Unless specifically directed by an instructor, there is no reason to have your phone out during lab. Please turn off and put away your phone before you arrive. Should your phone ring or be out during lab, you will be asked to put it away. On a second offense, you will be asked to leave and will receive a zero for that day's assignment.

6. <u>Academic Honesty</u> - As stated in the college catalogue and the Principles of Biology syllabus, "academic work is evaluated on the assumption that the work presented is the student's own." In lab, you are encouraged to work in pairs, but the report you turn in for a grade must represent your own work. If you have any questions about this requirement, please ask the laboratory coordinator for clarification.

LABORATORY SAFETY PROCEDURES

Any lab may be hazardous if materials or procedures are not handled properly. Safety procedures are necessary when you work with chemicals, glass, hot water, sharp instruments, open flames, etc. The following list of procedures is to be read, understood, and followed without exception for your own and others safety.

1. Notify faculty or staff of any accident such as the following:
    a. Spilling or splashing of any chemicals or liquid bacterial culture.
    b. Any breakage of a tube, Petri plate, etc. containing chemicals or live microorganisms.
    c. Any cuts, needle-sticks, eye-splashes or other physical injury during the lab.

2. Learn the location and proper usage of the eyewash fountain, fire extinguisher, safety shower, fire alarm box, evacuation routes, clean-up brush and dust pan, glass/chemical disposal can.

3. You cannot under any circumstances work alone in the lab.

4. Appropriate clothing must be worn in the lab. Shoes must be closed toe (no sandals) and pants must be knee length. Long hair should be tied back.

5. Gloves should be worn when working with bacteria and chemicals.

6. There will be absolutely no mouth-pipetting at any time, for any reason, in this laboratory.

7. Wash your hands thoroughly before and after each lab session.

8. Do not eat in the lab. Do not bring food nor beverages into the lab regardless of how they are packaged.

9. Do not taste or put things in your mouth, this includes pens and pencils.

10. Hang coats on the rack-not the backs of seats. Leave unnecessary books, etc. on the shelves provided and not at your work-space.

11. Do not heat a closed vessel. Always assume that plastic will melt so do not heat with a burner or autoclave.

12. Do not use equipment without proper training. Do not leave equipment running while you are out of the building. For example, do not put items in the autoclave and leave. Equipment timers have been known to fail so always stay close by when running.

13. Discard rules:
    a. Bacteria culture tubes upright in racks in the appropriate discard container.
    b. Petri plates upright in the appropriate discard container.
    d. Pipettes in pipette jars at your workbench.
    e. Microfuge tubes and micropipette tips in labeled beakers on benches.
    f. Agarose gels are to be thrown away in the "black boxes" located in Mur 210 and Graf 204.
    g. Sharps go into red sharps container not the trash.

14. Wearing a protective garment in the lab is always a good idea. It can be a lab coat, an old shirt, etc. It will protect you against microbial contamination and your clothes against spills and splashes.

15. Do not move gas cylinders unless you have been properly trained.

16. Return all material to their proper location. Keep sinks clean -- no cover slips, etc. in the drain. Return chairs under the bench when you leave lab.

Osmosis and Diffusion

Purpose
To understand the principles of osmosis and diffusion.

Objectives
After completing this lab, you should be able to:
- Describe the mechanism of diffusion.
- Describe a selectively permeable membrane and explain its role in osmosis.
- Explain diffusion and osmosis as it relates to cells.

Introduction
Cells must regulate the movement of molecules through the cytoplasm and across cellular membranes. The cytoplasm and extracellular environment of the cell are aqueous solutions, composed of water, which is the **solvent** and many organic and inorganic molecules, which are the **solutes**. Cellular membranes are selectively permeable, allowing water to pass freely but regulating the movement of molecules.

Diffusion is the process where water and selected small solutes move passively across the membrane from a region of high concentration to a region of low concentration. If nothing hinders diffusion the movement will continue until equilibrium is reached. **Osmosis** is a special case of diffusion, in which water diffuses across a selectively permeable membrane from an area of high concentration to an area of low concentration in an effort to reach an equal concentration on either side of the membrane.

The terms **hypertonic**, **hypotonic** and **isotonic** are used when comparing laboratory solutions to the solute concentration inside normal cells (Figure 1). A hypertonic solution has a higher solute concentration, a hypotonic solution has a lower solute concentration, and a isotonic solution has the same solute concentration found in the cells it is being compared with. There can be major consequences for cells depending on what type of solution they are exposed to, and this lab will explore the range of possibilities.

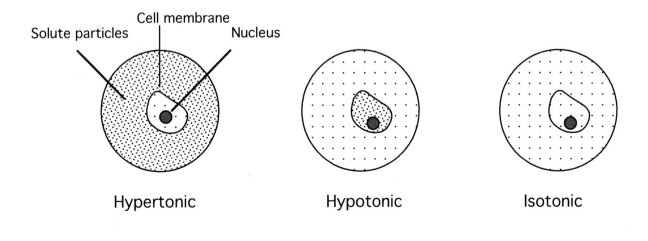

Figure 1

Estimating Osmolarity of Plant Cells

Sometimes the solute concentration of cells or the solutions they are bathed in is expressed by the term **osmolarity**, which is the total solute concentration expressed in terms of molarity. In the following experiments, you will estimate the osmolarity of potato cells by observing whether they gain or lose weight (water) when immersed in solutions of different osmolarity. Water will either diffuse into or out of the potato cells depending upon the osmolarity of the potato compared to the osmolarity of the solution it is immersed in.

Materials

Large potato, balance, 7 disposable cups, cork borer, scalpel, ruler
Sucrose solutions of different osmolarity: 0.0 (water), 0.1, 0.2, 0.3, 0.4, 0.5, 0.6 Molar (M)

Procedure

1. Label cups with the following: 0.0 M (water), 0.1 M, 0.2 M, 0.3 M, 0.4 M, 0.5 M, 0.6 M. Fill each cup about one third full with the appropriate sucrose solution.

2. Using a cork borer, cut 7 cylinders out of your potato. Cut the skin off each cylinder, and then cut each cylinder to the same length as the shortest cylinder.

3. Quickly and carefully, cut one potato cylinder into several approximately 2 mm slices. Cutting to a consistent disk width is important. It ensures each set of disks is comparable while increasing the potato surface area exposed to the solution.

4. Weigh the disks of the chopped cylinder. Record the weight in Table 1.

5. Place the slices next to the first solution. **DO NOT PUT THEM IN YET**. Repeat steps 3-4 for each of the remaining cylinders, placing each new set of disks next to a different solution.

6. Put each set of potato disks into its corresponding solution and let stand for approximately 90 minutes. Swirl the solution in the cups occasionally.

7. After incubation, remove the disks from solution and place them on a paper towel to drain briefly (do not blot).

8. Weigh each disk set. Record the weights in Table 1.

9. Compute the percentage (%) change in weight using the following formula:

% change in weight = (weight change/initial weight) X 100

Table 1. Sucrose Molarity

	0.0 M	0.1 M	0.2 M	0.3 M	0.4 M	0.5 M	0.6 M
Final Weight (g)							
Initial Weight (g)							
Weight Change (g)							
% Weight Change							

For Next Week

Graph the % change in weight vs. sucrose molarity for the seven sucrose solutions. At what sucrose molarity does the curve cross the zero-change point on the graph? How can this information be used to determine the sugar content of the potato?

NOTES

Determination of Enzyme Activity

Purpose
To understand basic protein structure
To understand basic enzyme kinetics
To understand homology between different enzymes in different species

Objectives
After completing the first portion of this lab, you should be able to:
- Identify the basic steps of an enzyme reaction
- Describe the purpose of an active site
- Perform serial dilutions to prepare substrates of different concentrations
- Set up an enzyme reaction
- Collect data using a spectrophotometer

After completing the second portion of this lab, you should be able to:
- Feel comfortable with all of the techniques attempted in Part 1
- Identify an enzyme in a solution using kinetic data

Introduction
In this laboratory we will be studying the organic molecule **acetylcholine**. Acetylcholine is produced in the neurons of animals, including humans, from the molecules acetyl coA and choline. Acetylcholine functions as a neurotransmitter, meaning that it can bind to receptors on different cell types and trigger neural activity. In the peripheral nervous system, it can stimulate muscle activity. In the central nervous system, it can have an inhibitory action on neurons.

Acetylcholine (or the very similar acetylthiocholine) can be broken down into two smaller molecules, thiocholine and acetate, as seen in the diagram below.

$$H_2O \; + \; (CH_3)_3N^+CH_2CH_2\text{-}S\text{-}CO\text{-}CH_3$$

(acetylthiocholine)

$$\downarrow$$

$$(CH_3)_3N^+CH_2CH_2\text{-}S^- \; + \; CH_3COO^- \; + \; 2H^+$$
(thiocholine)   *(acetate)*

The degradation reaction of acetylthiocholine into thiocholine and acetate as shown in this reaction happens at a very low rate. Thus, if neurons continue to make acetylcholine, and the acetylcholine breaks down at a very low rate, eventually the nervous system will have an excess concentration of acetylcholine. Proper nervous system function is extremely important, so organisms have developed complex systems of molecules and enzymes to regulate nervous system function.

To achieve the proper level of acetylcholine, the body must develop mechanisms for both quickly synthesizing and degrading this molecule. The reaction above takes a very long time to proceed, perhaps on the order of days, but your nervous system functions on the order of microseconds. To speed up the degradation reaction, your body uses a **catalyst** called an **enzyme** that can with some specificity catalyze the degradation of acetylcholine into choline and acetate.

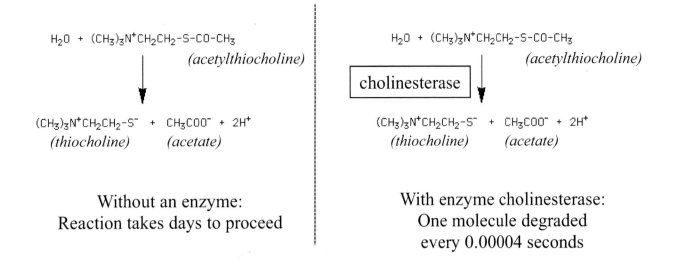

$$H_2O \; + \; (CH_3)_3N^+CH_2CH_2\text{-}S\text{-}CO\text{-}CH_3$$
(acetylthiocholine)

$$\downarrow$$

$$(CH_3)_3N^+CH_2CH_2\text{-}S^- \; + \; CH_3COO^- \; + \; 2H^+$$
(thiocholine)   *(acetate)*

Without an enzyme:
Reaction takes days to proceed

$$H_2O \; + \; (CH_3)_3N^+CH_2CH_2\text{-}S\text{-}CO\text{-}CH_3$$
(acetylthiocholine)

cholinesterase $\downarrow$

$$(CH_3)_3N^+CH_2CH_2\text{-}S^- \; + \; CH_3COO^- \; + \; 2H^+$$
(thiocholine)   *(acetate)*

With enzyme cholinesterase:
One molecule degraded
every 0.00004 seconds

Enzymes

In this laboratory, we will be investigating some of the properties of the protein molecules called **enzymes** which function in cells as biological catalysts. A catalyst is a substance that lowers the energy of activation for a reaction, without being chemically altered. Although the specific case of cholinesterase is illustrated in this laboratory, there are many different types of catalysts and there are many different mechanisms by which catalysts lower the energy of activation for a chemical reaction. Before we begin examining cholinesterases, we will first review the general principles behind enzymes, the most common type of catalyst found in biological systems.

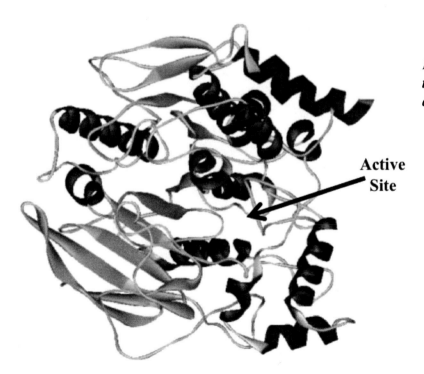

Active Site

Figure 1: Representation of the structure of the protein acetylcholinesterase.

As stated above, enzymes are proteins that act as catalysts. The temperatures found at the surface of the earth are ideal for maintaining the structure of proteins, membranes, and other macromolecular assemblies. However, without enzyme catalysts, most of the chemical reactions that occur in cells would proceed so slowly at these temperatures that they would take hundreds or thousands of years to reach equilibrium. Thus, enzymes make it possible for metabolic reactions to occur at temperatures where the structural components of cells are reasonably stable.

Enzymes are usually very specific with respect to the reactants that they interact with, they are active in small amounts, and they do not alter the equilibrium of the system. There are thousands of different enzymes found in any given cell and they catalyze thousands of different reactions by many different mechanisms. In a typical reaction, the starting reactant(s) or **substrate(s)** undergoes a chemical change and is converted into a **product.** Each enzyme has a unique chemical structure and shape that allows it to catalyze a very specific chemical reaction.

Most, but not all enzymes are named after their substrate(s), with the suffix **"ase"** at the end of the name. The names of enzymes also usually include some reference to the type of reaction (e.g. esterase, isomerase, etc.). Some exceptions to this rule include the digestive enzymes trypsin, chymotrypsin, acrosin, thrombin, and pepsin.

Each enzyme shows **specificity** because its shape, structure, and charge is such that it will only interact with a specific substrate or with molecules that closely resemble the substrate. The enzyme combines with the substrate to form an **enzyme-substrate complex (ES)**. The substrate is then converted to product, leaving an **enzyme-product complex (EP),** the product dissociates from the enzyme, and the enzyme is ready to interact with another molecule of substrate:

$$E + S \Longleftrightarrow ES \Longleftrightarrow EP \Longleftrightarrow E + P$$

The property that most enzymes have in common is that they are polymers of amino acids. Each enzyme has a substrate-binding site, called the **active site,** located within folds at the surface of the protein. Below is a schematic of the acetylcholinesterase active site (figure 2). When a molecule of substrate binds to the active site of an enzyme, it distorts the shape of the enzyme. The distorted enzyme in turn places stress on the chemical bonds of the substrate, thereby increasing the probability of the bonds breaking and reforming. If two reactants are involved, they are brought together in space when they bind to the active site. The enzyme performs the same function as a high energy collision: it brings the reactants together in space at just the right angle and places stress on the chemical bonds. Consequently, an enzyme increases the probability of a chemical reaction and eliminates the need to add energy in the form of heat to achieve activation. Enzymes usually bind to substrates through weak interactions such as ionic bonding, hydrogen bonding, Van der Waals forces, and hydrophobic interactions. Some enzymes actually form covalent bonds with substrates during intermediate stages of a reaction.

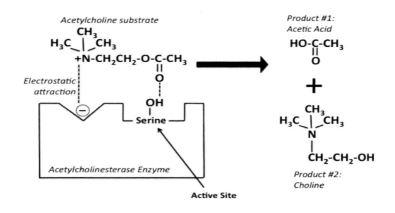

Figure 2: Enzyme: substrate interaction of acetylcholinesterase and acetylcholine. Acetylcholine is attracted to the active site through electrostatic forces. Interaction with the serine residue (amino acid) exerts stress on the bond and results in the production of two products: acetic acid and choline.

Many factors influence the rate of product formation in an enzyme-catalyzed reaction. For example, when the concentration of substrate is increased, the rate of the reaction increases. There is a point when increasing the concentration of substrate will saturate all of the available enzyme active sites and the rate of reaction will no longer increase. This point is called the **maximal velocity, or Vmax**. At Vmax, the rate of the reaction can only be increased by adding more enzyme. Vmax represents the maximum amount of substrate that can react in one minute (moles of substrate/min) and is a measure of the ability of an enzyme to catalyze a reaction (**catalytic efficiency**).

Factors that influence the structure of an enzyme will often affect the ability of an enzyme to catalyze a reaction. Increasing **temperature** increases the rate of all chemical reactions. Beyond a temperature specific to each enzyme, however, enzymes lose their ability to catalyze reactions because heat induces changes in their tertiary or quaternary structures. Other factors that can alter enzyme structures include the **pH** (hydrogen ion concentration) of a solution, **ionic strength** of a solution (the concentration of dissolved ions), and **divalent cations** such as calcium or magnesium.

Biochemists use two important parameters when studying enzymes: the ability of the substrate to bind to the active site (sometimes called enzyme-substrate affinity), and the catalytic efficiency (Vmax). Factors such as temperature, pH, ionic strength, and inhibitors can alter these parameters and give important clues concerning the properties and regulation of a particular enzyme.

Catalysis by Cholinesterases

In the enzymatic mechanism of cholinesterase shown in figure 3, you can see that three amino acids (also known as the catalytic triad) are involved in catalysis by cholinesterases. In the case of acetylcholinesterase (AChE), these amino acids of the enzyme are the glutamate (glu), histidine (his), and the serine (ser) in the active site.

First, a covalent bond is formed between the acetyl group of the substrate and serine. Next, the bond between acetate and choline is broken and choline is released. Finally, the covalent bond between serine and the acetate portion of the substrate is broken, forming acetate that is released from the enzyme, and returning serine to its original state so that it is available for a new round of catalysis. Through this movement of electrons glutamate activates histidine, which in turn activates serine so it can attack the acetyl group of the substrate.

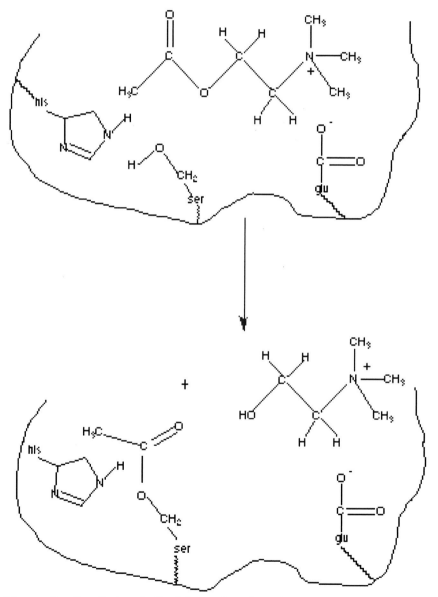

Figure 3: Catalytic triad of the active site of acetylcholinesterase *This diagram of the active site of acetylcholinesterase identifies the three residues (amino acids serine, glutamate, and histidine) that perform the chemistry of converting acetylcholine into acetic acid and choline. See the text above for more detail on the enzymatic mechanism.*

Enzyme Action: Cholinesterases

All jawed vertebrates possess two evolutionarily related **cholinesterases** (ChEs) as the result of a gene duplication event early in vertebrate evolution. One of these ChEs is **acetylcholinesterase** (AChE), which hydrolyzes the neurotransmitter acetylcholine (ACh) into acetate and choline at the neuromuscular junction and at many synapses in the central and peripheral nervous system, and terminates the action of the neurotransmitter; at the neuromuscular junction, this hydrolysis allows the relaxation of skeletal muscle.

The other ChE is **butyrylcholinesterase** (BuChE). BuChE is widely distributed in many tissues, with particularly high levels present in the liver. Despite the fact that BuChE has been studied for well over 50 years, its function remains uncertain. Certain humans appear to lack the enzyme yet appear to be normal. However, it is now widely thought to be involved in detoxification systems in animals, hydrolyzing natural toxins that may be ingested.

Table 1. Characteristics of Vertebrate Cholinesterases.

Characteristic	*Vertebrate AChE*	*Vertebrate BuChE*
Substrate Specificity		
Acetylcholine (ACh)	Yes	Yes
Butyrylcholine (BuCh)	No	Yes

Substrate Specificity. As outlined in Table 1, AChE hydrolyzes ACh almost exclusively, while BuChE is capable of hydrolyzing both ACh and butyrylcholine (BuCh) at least as well. Thus, substrate specificity can be used to distinguish between the two enzymes.

One should note that while ACh is a natural substrate present in vertebrates, BuCh is a synthetic compound - it does not exist in nature and is not a neurotransmitter but is used in enzymatic studies. BuCh is a larger choline ester than ACh as a result of its three-carbon, butryryl acyl group in place of the one-carbon, acetyl acyl group of ACh. The structures of ACh and BuCh are shown in Fig. 4. Note that the two structures are identical except for the acyl groups located at the left side of the molecules (-CH3 for ACh and –CH2CH2CH3 for BuCh). In fact, this and other results indicate that BuChE has a larger active site than AChE and is able to accommodate a relatively wide variety of substrates; it is not nearly as specific as AChE. For example, BuChE can hydrolyze aspirin, cocaine, and heroin.

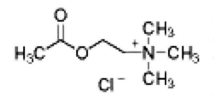

Figure 4 Structures of acetylcholine and butyrylcholine. Acetylcholine is at the top and butyrylcholine at the bottom. Acetylcholine is smaller while butyrylcholine is longer and bulkier. This difference in size makes them fit differently as substrates in the active site of an enzyme.

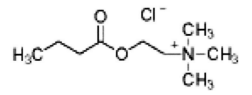

<u>Refer to Figure 1 (page 8) to answer the following questions.</u>

1. Using your knowledge from lecture and the textbook, identify the type of structure depicted by the dark coils in Figure 1.

_____

2. Using your knowledge from lecture and the textbook, identify the type of structure depicted by the flat ribbons in Figure 1.

_____

3. What is the name of the monomer that polymerizes to create a protein? _____

4. In your own words, describe what you would find in an active site. _____

_____

_____

5. Why is the enzyme activity of cholinesterases important? _____

_____

_____

6. Identify each of the following as either a substrate or an enzyme:

Acetylcholinesterase (AChE) _____

Acetylcholine _____

Acetylthiocholine _____

Butyrylcholinesterase (BuChE) _____

Butyrylcholine _____

Butyrylthiocholine _____

7. If you were given each of the two substrates described above, acetylcholine (ACh) and butyrylcholine (BuCh), would you expect acetylcholinesterase (AChE) to catalyze their degradation reactions? Why or why not? Would you expect butyrylcholinesterase (BuChE) to catalyze their degradation reactions? Why or why not?

PART ONE EXPERIMENTAL PROCEDURE

CATALYSIS BY CHOLINESTERASES

Quite often, natural substrates and products are difficult to assay (measure or quantify) without laborious analytical procedures. Accordingly, biochemists often use artificial substrates or products that are colored and therefore easy to detect and measure. For instance, if a colored substrate were used, the reaction could be monitored by disappearance of color as the substrate was converted to product. Conversely, the appearance of a colored product could also be monitored. In other cases, biochemists use coupled reactions, where the product of a reaction itself reacts with a second compound that produces a colored product. An example of the last case is the Ellman esterase assay (Ellman et al., 1961), which is virtually the only assay used for ChEs at the present tme. In the Ellman assay, **acyl*thio*choline esters**, rather than acyl*oxy*choline esters are used as substrates. Hydrolysis of the acylthiocholine substrates (e.g. acetylthiocholine or butyrylthiocholine) produces thiocholine which in turn reacts with a color reagent **dithiobis-nitrobenzoic acid (DTNB)**, liberating the yellow colored **5-thio-2-nitrobenzoate ion** (Fig. 5).We will measure the amount of 5-thio-2-nitrobenzoate ion present using a spectrophotometer. Each thiocholine product produced reacts with a DTNB molecule so there is an exact one to one correspondence in the concentration of both products.

Figure 5. Color assay for cholinesterases. *In this reaction, acetylcholine is hydrolyzed to acetate and thiocholine. Thiocholine reacts with DTNB producing the yellow colored 5-thio- 2-nitrobenzoate ion.*

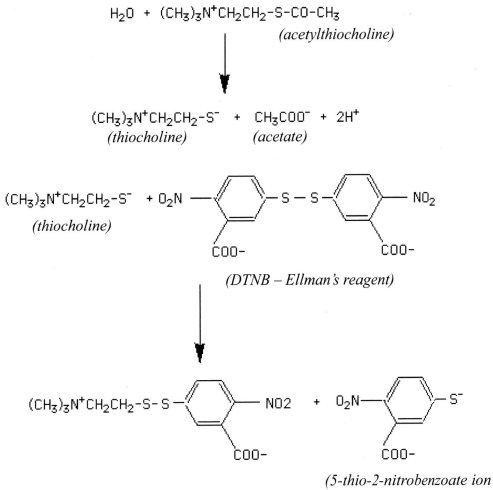

11

Acetlycholinesterase or Butyrylcholinesterase?

During this week's experiments, each lab group will test the ability of one enzyme to hydrolyze each of the two substrates. For example, your group may receive acetylcholinesterase (AChE), and you will test the substrates acetylthiocholine (ASCh) and butyrylthiocholine (BuSCh). Alternatively, your group may receive butyrylcholinesterase (BuChE) and test those same substrates, acetylthiocholine and butyrylthiocholine. At the end of the lab period, groups will confer, and we will determine the substrate specificity for each enzyme.

Variables used in an experiment are termed either the "**dependent variable**" or "**independent variable**". The "dependent variable" represents the output or effect. The "independent variables" represent the inputs or causes. Other variables may also be observed for various reasons. As you read these instructions and perform the experiments, think about what the dependent and independent variables are.

The sections below detail the procedure for setting up a reaction using the substrate acetylthiocholine (Hydrolysis I) or butyrylthiocholine (Hydrolysis II). In the tables, you will use your assigned enzyme wherever the designation "Enzyme (E)" occurs.

EFFECT OF SUBSTRATE CONCENTRATION ON RATE OF HYDROLYSIS I: HYDROLYSIS OF ACETYLTHIOCHOLINE

Serial Dilution of Substrate Stock Solution

You will be given a solution of **20 mM acetylthiocholine (ASCh)** in sodium phosphate buffer. In five labeled test tubes (S1-S5), make a 1:2 serial dilution of the substrate as described below to prepare substrate solutions at five different concentrations. Store these test tubes in a rack.

1. Pipette 1 ml of sodium phosphate buffer into tubes S2-S5.
2. Transfer all (approximately 1.7 ml) the 20 mM ASCh into tube S1.
3. Transfer 1 ml of the 20 mM ASCh in tube S1 into tube S2. **Mix well**. This 1:2 dilution yields an ASCh concentration of 10 mM in tube S2.
4. Transfer 1 ml of the 10 mM ASCh in tube S2 into tube 3. **Mix well**. This 1:2 dilution yields an ASCh concentration of 5 mM in tube S3.
5. Continue for all the tubes. The last tube will contain 2 ml of solution.
6. Calculate and record the ASCh concentrations below and in your notebook.

Tube #	S1	S2	S3	S4	S5
Substrate (ASCh) concentration	20mM	10mM			

Once the first two or three steps to making the serial dilution are complete, open your laptop. Your spectrophotometer is connected and the Logger Pro program is running. You should see tables and a large graph on the screen.

Spectrophotometer Calibration

When all five tubes of the serial dilution have been prepared, using a serological pipette, transfer 2.4 ml of Ellman's Solution into one of your cuvettes. Be careful, cuvettes tip over easily. Then, using a micropipettor, transfer 0.3 ml of the solution in tube S1 into to cuvette. You will be shown how to mix the contents of a cuvette using parafilm. Insert the cuvette into the spectrophotometer with the clear, smooth sides of the cuvette in the light path and follow the instructions given to calibrate the spectrophotometer. Once calibration is complete, remove and set aside the cuvette, it will serve as your first reaction cuvette (see table below).

Assembly of Reaction
The contents of your five reaction cuvettes are shown in the table below. Your calibration cuvette will serve as 1E (it only needs enzyme added). Fill out the table before proceeding.

Cuvette	Stock [Substrate] mM	ml Substrate Solution	ml Ellman's Solution	ml Enzyme (E)	Total Final Volume	Final [Substrate] mM
1 E	20	0.3	2.4	*Zero, then 0.3*	3.0	2
2 E	10	0.3	2.4	0.3	3.0	1
3 E		0.3	2.4	0.3	3.0	
4 E		0.3	2.4	0.3	3.0	
5 E		0.3	2.4	0.3	3.0	

IMPORTANT: Do NOT add enzyme to a cuvette until you are ready to start the reaction.

Collecting Data

1. During the data collection process, assign one person to run the computer software, one to pipette Ellman's Solution and handle the cuvettes, one to pipette Substrate Solutions, and one to add enzyme when the time is appropriate.

2. Begin with tube 1E (your calibration tube). Add the appropriate volume of enzyme to the cuvette using the micropipette, cover the top with parafilm, and invert to mix.

3. Immediately insert the cuvette into the spectrophotometer with the clear sides of the cuvette in the light path. The direction of the light path is marked by an arrow.

4. Press the green START button on the laptop screen's upper right side. It will turn into a red STOP button when pressed.

5. The program will collect a data point every second for 120 seconds. DO NOT remove the cuvette while data is being collected.

6. While this reaction is in the spectrophotometer, you can begin preparing tube 2E by adding Ellman's Solution and the appropriate Substrate Solution to a clean cuvette.

7. After 120 seconds, the run is complete, and the red STOP button turns back into the green START button. Remove the cuvette and set it aside. You will need to rinse your cuvettes with deionized water between usages.

8. In the "Experiment" pull-down menu, select "Store Latest Run". You are ready for the cuvette 2E run. Go to Step 2 and repeat this process for tubes 2E-5E.

9. When all five runs are complete, you will be shown how to save your data as a pdf.

EFFECT OF SUBSTRATE CONCENTRATION ON RATE OF HYDROLYSIS II: HYDROLYSIS OF BUTYRYLTHIOCHOLINE

Serial Dilution of Substrate Stock Solution

In labeled test tubes, make a 1:2 serial dilution of the substrate as shown below to prepare stock solutions of substrate at different concentrations.

NOTE: You are repeating the last experiment; however, this time you are using the substrate BuSCh. You will be given a solution of **20 mM BuSCh** in sodium phosphate buffer.

1. Pipette 1 ml of sodium phosphate buffer into tubes S2-S5.
2. Transfer all (approximately 1.7 ml) the 20 mM BuSCh into tube S1.
3. Transfer 1 ml of the 20 mM BuSCh in tube 1 into tube 2. **Mix well.** This 1:2 dilution yields a BuSCh concentration of 10 mM.
4. Transfer 1 ml of the 10 mM BuSCh in tube 2 into tube 3. **Mix well.** This 1:2 dilution yields a BuSCh concentration of 5 mM.
5. Continue for all the tubes. The last tube will contain 2 ml of solution.
6. Calculate and record the BuSCh concentrations below.

Tube #	S1	S2	S3	S4	S5
Substrate (BuSCh) concentration	20mM	10mM			

Assembly of Reaction

The contents of your five new reaction cuvettes are shown in the table below. **You need not re-calibrate your spectrophotometer.** Fill out the table before proceeding to the data collection protocol you followed previously.

Cuvette	Stock [Substrate] mM	ml Substrate Solution	ml Ellman's Solution	ml Enzyme (E)	Total Final Volume	Final [Substrate] mM
1 E	20	0.3	2.4	0.3	3.0	2
2 E	10	0.3	2.4	0.3	3.0	1
3 E		0.3	2.4	0.3	3.0	
4 E		0.3	2.4	0.3	3.0	
5 E		0.3	2.4	0.3	3.0	

PART TWO EXPERIMENTAL DESIGN

DETERMINATION OF ENZYME TYPE IN AN UNKNOWN SAMPLE

The ChE enzyme solution that you will test was made by dilution of horse serum in sodium phosphate buffer (pH 7.0). **The goal of this experiment is to determine whether it is AChE or BuChE.** All vertebrate AChEs/BuChEs are similar, and all mammalian AChEs/BuChEs are highly conserved. Thus, what is true for horse serum ChE, whether it is AChE or BuChE can be generalized to other AChEs and BuChEs, particularly mammalian, including human.

You will be given horse serum and use the same equipment (laptop, spectrophotometer, pipettes, etc) from Part 1. Before beginning your experiment, prepare a detailed, **efficient** protocol to determine the nature of the cholinesterase present in the horse serum. Use what you have learned in previous labs and in lecture to design your experiment. Once you have a protocol, present it to a TA or Instructor. You will be asked to describe your plan's rationale and for a list of reagents (enzymes, substrates, other solutions, etc) you will require.

NOTES

Photosynthesis

Purpose:
To understand the principle of photosynthesis.

Objectives:
After completing this lab, you should be able to:
*   State the summary equation for photosynthesis.
*   State the separate sets of reactions involved in photosynthesis.
*   Separate photosynthetic pigments.

Introduction:
Photosynthesis is unquestionably the most important series of chemical reactions that occur on Earth. Most life is totally dependent on photosynthesis for food and oxygen! This includes almost all heterotrophs, including humans. Photosynthesis is a complex chemical process that converts radiant energy (light) to chemical energy (glucose). A summary equation for photosynthesis is presented below:

$$6CO_2 + 12H_2O \xrightarrow[\text{chlorophyll}]{\text{light}} C_6H_{12}O_6 + 6H_2O + 6O_2$$

CARBON   WATER   GLUCOSE   WATER   OXYGEN
DIOXIDE

Thus, photosynthesis is the light and chlorophyll-dependent conversion of carbon dioxide and water to glucose, water, and oxygen. Oxygen is released to the environment, and glucose is typically stored as **starch**, a polysaccharide.

Photosynthesis can be divided into two main sets of reactions. Some characteristics of these reactions are compared below:

LIGHT REACTIONS	LIGHT INDEPENDENT REACTIONS CALVIN CYCLE
Light dependent	Light independent
Water splits to release oxygen, electrons, and protons: ATP (energy source) and NADPH (reducing power) generated for use in Calvin Cycle.	Carbon dioxide reduced to glucose using products of light reactions; ADP and NADP regenerated.

16

Paper Chromatography of Photosynthetic Pigments

Light must be absorbed before its energy can be utilized. A substance that absorbs light is called a **pigment**. The green pigment in plant cells that absorbs light for photosynthesis is **chlorophyll.** However, chlorophyll is not the only photosynthetic pigment. **Accessory pigments** such as *carotenes and xanthophylls* also absorb light for photosynthesis. The light energy absorbed by accessory pigments is transmitted to chlorophyll, which is the primary photosynthetic pigment.

Paper chromatography is a technique for separating dissolved compounds, in this case chlorophyll, carotene, and xanthophyll present in photosynthetic cells. When a solution of these pigments is applied to strips of paper, the pigments adsorb onto the cellulose fibers of the paper. When the tip of the paper is immersed in a solvent, the solvent is absorbed and moves through the paper. As the solvent moves through the spot where the mixture of pigments was applied to the paper, the pigments will dissolve in the moving solvent. However, the pigments can't keep up with the moving solvent--some pigments will move almost as fast as the solvent, while others will move more slowly. This differential movement of pigments is the result of each pigment having a characteristic tendency to stick (i.e. be adsorbed) to the cellulose fibers of the paper. A pigment's molecular size, polarity, and solubility determine the strength of this tendency. Pigments strongly adsorbed move slowly; pigments weakly adsorbed move faster. Thus, each pigment has a characteristic rate of movement, meaning the relationship of the distance moved by a pigment to the distance moved by the solvent front is specific for a given set of conditions. We call this relationship the *Rf*, and define it as follows:

Rf = (Distance moved by pigment)/(Distance moved by solvent)

Thus, paper chromatography can be used to identify each pigment by its characteristic Rf.

Materials

Chromatography jars	Heater/hair dryer
Chromatography paper (Whatman's #1)	Capillary tubes
Plant extract	Rulers
Chromatography solution (9:1 solution of petroleum ether and acetone)	

Procedure:

1. Observe the contents of the flask labeled *Plant Extract*. Since it is green, you've probably concluded one of its major constituents is chlorophyll. That's correct, but other pigments are also present. You'll separate these pigments via paper chromatography.

2. Chromatography solution has been poured into the chromatography jar to a depth of approximately 1.0 cm. Let it sit while you prepare your sample for analysis.
   NOTE: This solvent is highly flammable so extinguish all flames, hot plates, etc before working with the solvent.

3. Obtain a strip of chromatography paper. Handle the paper by the edge because the smallest amount of oil will affect the results.

4. Make a faint line with a pencil 1.5 cm from the end of the strip.

5. Using a capillary tube filled with the plant extract, make line of extract on the pencil line about 0.5 cm from either side of the paper strip. Allow the line to dry and then repeat until 20 lines have been spotted. The line should be **dark** green.

6. Remove the lid from the chromatography jar. The jar should have about 1 cm of solvent in the bottom. Roll the paper into a cylinder and place in the jar.

7. Replace the lid. Be sure you can see solvent moving. Watch carefully.

8. When the solvent front reaches 0.5 cm from the top of the paper (in about 5-7 minutes), remove the strip and *quickly mark the solvent front with a pencil.* **Do not let the solvent front run off the end of the paper.** Set strip aside and allow to air dry.

Results

1. You'll see four bands of color on the strip--a yellow band of *carotenes* near the top, followed by a yellow band of *xanthophylls*, a blue-green band of *chlorophyll a*, and a yellow-green band of *chlorophyll b* near the bottom.

2. Draw what you see and calculate the Rf for each of these pigments.

	Solvent front	**Pigment**	**Rf**
		Carotenes	————
		Xanthophylls	————
		Chlorophyll a	————
		Chlorophyll b	————
	Pigment origin		

18

Oxygen Production During Photosynthesis (splitting H₂O during light reaction)

Since oxygen is a by-product of photosynthesis, its production is an indirect indicator of photosynthesis. In this demonstration, a cut plant sprig is submerged inverted in a sodium bicarbonate solution and placed under a light source. Observe the oxygen bubbles produced. Are you certain these bubbles are the result of photosynthesis? How could you test this?

Electron Transport in Chloroplasts in the Light Reaction

Photochemical reactions in photosynthesis involve the transfer of electrons between various compounds. In 1937, Robin Hill demonstrated that isolated chloroplasts will perform this electron transfer in the absence of carbon dioxide if provided with an alternate or artificial electron acceptor other than carbon dioxide. This observation indicated that electron transport does not require carbon dioxide fixation to occur. That is, electron transfer and carbon dioxide fixation occur by separate sets of reactions. Electron transfer can be detected using a dye called 2,6-dichlorophenol-indolephenol (DCPIP). In its oxidized, state DCPIP is blue. Upon accepting electrons (reduced), DCPIP becomes colorless.

Materials
0.2 mM DCPIP	Fresh plant extract	0.1 M Phosphate buffer pH 6.5
Test tubes & rack	Desk lamp	Aluminum foil

Table 1. Solutions for Observation of Electron Flow

Tube	Chloroplast extract	PO₄ Buffer	H₂O	2 µM DCPIP	Final Volume
1	0.5 mL	3 mL	0.5 mL	1 mL	5 mL
2		3 mL			5 mL
3		3 mL			5 mL
4		3 mL			5 mL

What do you hypothesize will happen if you mix the ingredients listed for Tube 1 above?

What controls do you need to run to properly test your hypothesis? Complete the table for up to five tubes to test your hypothesis. You may decrease the volume of chloroplast extract and DCPIP, but make sure that you increase the volume of water by the corresponding amount to have the final volume remain at 5 ml.

When you have completed the table, add all ingredients into labeled tubes, mix well, and place approximately 0.5 m in front of a desk lamp.

Observe and describe your results.

NOTES

Microscopy

Objectives
After completing this lab, you should be able to identify the parts of the compound microscope and understand how to use it correctly.

Cells are below the limit of resolution of the human eye; thus, we must use a microscope to study them. There are two types of microscopes used in biology: **light** and **electron**. We will use only light microscopes today. It is important to master the techniques you learn today because you will use them in almost every biology course you take at Linfield and, probably, throughout your career as a biologist.

Parts of the Compound Microscope
There are several different kinds of light microscope, such as phase-contrast, dark-field, polarizing, and UV. They differ in the source and manner by which light is passed through the specimen. We will use a binocular light microscope in this and other labs during the semester.

Procedure
Obtain a microscope. Observe as your TA demonstrates the proper carrying technique. *Always use two hands*: hold the arm with one hand and support the base with the other. Remove the cover but do not plug in the microscope. Use Fig. 1 to identify the microscope parts.

- The **head** supports two sets of magnifying lenses. The **ocular** is the lens in the **eyepieces**. It has a magnification of 10x. A **pointer** is located in one eyepiece and used to point to an object in the **field of view**, the circle of light seen when looking through the oculars.

- **Objectives** are the four lenses on the **revolving nosepiece**. The shortest lens, called the **scanning lens**, is 4x. Higher power lenses are 10x, 40x and 100x. The 100x lens is called the **oil immersion lens** and will be used later.

- The **arm** supports the stage and condenser lens. The **condenser lens** is used to focus light from the lamp through the specimen. The height of the condenser is adjusted by turning the **adjustment knob**. The **iris diaphragm** controls the width of the circle of light (aperture) and, therefore, the amount of light passing through the specimen.

- The **stage** supports the specimen. Two stage adjustment knobs can move the specimen right and left and back and forth. The distance between the stage and an objective lens is adjusted with the **coarse** and **fine focus adjustment knobs**.

- The **base** acts as a stand for the microscope and houses the **light source**. The intensity of the light that passes through the specimen is adjusted with the **light intensity lever**. In general, more light is needed when using high power than when using low power lenses.

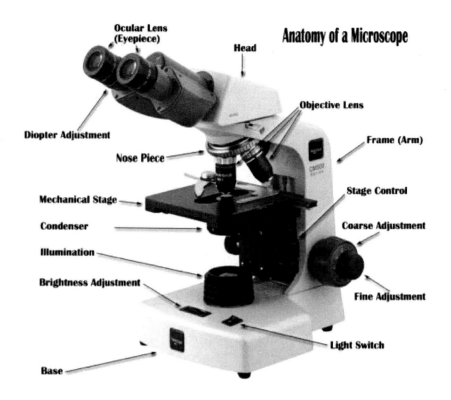

Anatomy of a Microscope

Ocular Lens (Eyepiece)

Head

Objective Lens

Diopter Adjustment

Frame (Arm)

Nose Piece

Mechanical Stage

Stage Control

Condenser

Coarse Adjustment

Illumination

Brightness Adjustment

Fine Adjustment

Light Switch

Base

Basic Microscope Techniques

1. **Adjusting the focus on your microscope**

   a. Plug your microscope into the outlet.

   b. Adjust the light intensity to mid-range.

   c. Rotate the 4x objective into position using the revolving nosepiece ring, not the objective itself. Slides should be placed on and removed from the stage *only when the 4x objective is in place*. Removing a slide when a higher objective is in position may scratch the lens or break the slide.

   d. Place the newsprint slide on the stage and center the specimen over the stage opening.

   e. Look through the ocular and bring the type into rough focus by slowly moving the coarse adjustment upward or downward.

   f. Adjust your **interpupillary distance** and **diopter**:

   - While looking through both eyepieces, hold the **slides** to the right and left of the eyepiece tubes with both hands and push the tubes together or pull them apart laterally until perfect binocular vision is obtained.

   - Record the value (in mm) of your interpupillary distance in the space below: This can be read from a scale just to the left of the right eyepiece.

   - While keeping your right eye closed and looking only through the left eyepiece, rotate the **tube length adjustment ring** on the left eyepiece to bring the typeface into focus.

   - Now, while looking through both eyepieces, the typeface should be in focus. Also, you should see an **ocular micrometer** and **pointer** in your field of view. *Notify your TA before proceeding if you have any problems.*

g. Rotate the 10x objective lens into position.

h. Look through the ocular and slowly focus upward with the coarse adjustment knob until the image is in rough focus. Sharpen the focus using the fine adjustment knob.

i. You can increase or decrease the contrast by adjusting the iris diaphragm opening. Adjust the opening until the image is sharp. Note that too much light decreases contrast and actually may make viewing an object more difficult.

j. Move the slide slowly to the right.

In what direction does the image in the ocular move? _____

Is the image in the ocular inverted relative to the specimen on the stage? _____

k. Center the specimen in the field of view. Rotate the 40x objective into position while watching from the side. If it appears the objective will hit the slide, stop and ask for assistance.

l. After the 40x objective lens is in place, focus using the fine adjustment knob. *Never focus with the coarse adjustment knob when you are using the high-power objective.*

m. The distance between the specimen and the objective lens is called the **working distance**.

Is this distance greater with the 40x or the 10x objective? _____

Looking at the newsprint, is it readable or is the image inverted? _____

2. **Focusing and understanding inversion**

a. Adjust the light intensity to mid-range.

b. Rotate the 4x objective into position using the revolving nosepiece ring, not the objective itself. Slides should be placed on and removed from the stage *only when the 4x objective is in place*. Removing a slide with a higher objective in position may scratch the lens or break the slide.

c. Place the "letter e" slide on the stage and center the specimen over the stage opening.

d. Look through the ocular and bring the letter into rough focus by slowly moving the coarse adjustment upward or downward.

e. Rotate the 10x objective lens into position.

f. Optimize the position of the iris as described above.

g. Look through the ocular and slowly focus upward with the coarse adjustment knob until the image is in rough focus. Sharpen the focus using the fine adjustment knob.

h. You can increase or decrease the contrast by adjusting the iris diaphragm opening. Adjust the opening until the image is sharp. Note that too much light decreases contrast and actually may make viewing an object more difficult.

i. Center the specimen in the field of view. Rotate the 40x objective into position while watching from the side. If it appears the objective will hit the slide, stop and ask for assistance.

j. After the 40x objective lens is in place, focus using the fine adjustment knob. *Never focus with the coarse adjustment knob when you are using the high-power objective.*

k. Is the letter e on your slide readable or inverted? What does this tell you about how the "letter e" specimen was mounted on the slide?

3. **For each specimen drawn, you will calculate and record its actual size and magnification.**

   Actual size calculation:

   a. First, compute the **power** used to view the specimen by multiplying the power of the ocular lens by that of the objective lens. _____

   b. Use the following chart to calculate the **actual size** of a specimen.

Power (ocular x objective)	Value of each ocular micrometer unit (mm)	Approximate field of view (diameter in mm)
10 X 4= 40X	0.03	4.0
10 X 10= 100X	0.01	1.9
10 X 40= 400X	0.003	0.40
10 X 100= 1000X	0.001	0.19

   c. If a cell you are viewing using the 4x objective measures 5 ocular units, calculate its actual size: _____

   d. What is the relationship between the power and the size of the field of view? _____

4. **The depth of field is the thickness of the specimen that may be seen in focus at one time. Because the depth of focus is very short in the compound microscope, one may need to focus up and down to view all planes of a specimen.**

   a. Rotate the 4x objective into position and place the thread slide on the stage. Center the slide so that the region where the threads cross is in the center of the stage opening.

   b. Adjust the light so that you have good contrast for fibers in the threads.

   c. Focus on the region where the threads cross.

      Are all the threads in focus at the same time?_____

   d. Rotate the 10x objective into position and focus on the cross.

      Are all the threads in focus at the same time?_____

   e. Focus upward until the threads are just out of focus. Slowly focus down using the fine adjustment.

      Which thread comes into focus first?_____

      Is this thread lying under or over the other threads?_____

   f. Rotate the 40x objective into position and slowly focus up and down, using the fine adjustment only.

      Does the 10x or 40x objective have a shorter depth of field?_____

Mitosis

Purpose
To gain an understanding of mitosis and meiosis using bead models and prepared slides.

Objectives
After completing this lab, you should be able to:
- Explain the steps of mitosis using the bead model.
- Be able to identify the stages of mitosis from microscope slides

Supporting material in textbook
Chapters 12 and 13 contain information about mitosis. In particular, note Figures 12.4 (p.220), 12.5 (p.221), 12.6 (p.222), 13.8 (p.244).

Introduction
The nuclei in cells of eukaryotic organisms contain **chromosomes** with clusters of **genes**, discrete units of hereditary information consisting of double-stranded deoxyribonucleic acid (DNA). When cells divide, chromosomes are duplicated and passed on to daughter cells. Multicellular organisms have **reproductive cells** (eggs and sperm) as wells as **somatic (body) cells**.

In somatic cells, as well as unicellular organisms, the nucleus divides by **mitosis** into two daughter nuclei. Each daughter nucleus has the same number of chromosomes and the same genes as the parent cell. In **diploid (2n)** organisms, there are two copies of each chromosome, that is, the chromosomes exist as **homologous pairs.** In **haploid (1n)** cells, each chromosome is represented only once. For example, human cells contain 23 different chromosomes (1n = 23), so diploid human cells contain a total of 46 chromosomes (2n = 46) – 23 pairs of homologous chromosomes. Homologous chromosomes are similar in that they are the same size and contain the same genes, but they are not identical because each chromosome of a given pair may contain a different **allele** of the same gene. For example, chromosome one may carry the eye color gene, but one of the homologous pairs may carry the blue color allele and the other may carry the brown color allele. Blue and brown are different alleles of one gene, the gene for eye color. Incidentally, the individual in the example above would be **heterozygous** for the eye color gene, because s/he carries different alleles on each chromosome of the homologous chromosome one pair. If the above individual carried two identical eye color alleles, one on each of the homologues, s/he would be termed **homozygous** for the eye color gene. Since mitosis is a form of **clonal reproduction**, if the parent cell was diploid, the daughter cells will be diploid. It should be noted that if the parent cell were haploid, for example as in bacteria and fungi, the daughter cell also will be haploid.

Modeling Mitosis

Materials
Colored beads with magnetic centromeres

Procedure
Make two chromosomes of beads, each chromosome should be 14 beads long with a centromere in the middle. One of the chromosomes should be red and the other should be pink. This is your **homologous pair** of chromosomes.

G1 phase of the cell cycle

- Pile the chromosomes into the center of your nucleus. You can use chalk to draw a nucleus on the bench.

S (synthesis) phase of the cell cycle

- **Replicate** your two chromosomes. Replication leads to **identical** copies so your beads must be the same color after replication. Both chromosomes must be replicated. **Important:** replicated chromosomes remain **joined at the centromere.**

- You should now have two chains of beads for **each** chromosome--four chromosomes total. Each pair of **replicated chromosomes** should be joined together at the centromere. The replicated chromosomes are called **sister chromatids.**

G2 phase of the cell cycle

- The cell is continuing its regular cell activities and is preparing for mitosis.

M (mitosis) phase of the cell cycle

Prophase. The first stage of mitosis.

a. Prophase begins when chromosomes begin to coil and condense.

b. Nuclear envelope breaks down. Erase your chalk nuclear membrane.

c. Spindles form. Draw a spindle with chalk on your bench. One spindle fiber from each pole becomes associated with the centromere (actually it is called a **kinetochore** at this time) of each pair of sister chromatids.

Metaphase. Replicated chromosomes line up in the middle of the cell.

a. During mitosis, the replicated chromosomes line up in a single column. The column is oriented perpendicular to the spindle poles. **This arrangement is an important difference between mitosis and meiosis.**

Anaphase. Sister chromatids begin to separate and move towards the poles.

a. Separate your sister chromatids **at the centromere** and move each of them to a different pole. **The way in which the chromosomes separate during metaphase is another important difference between mitosis and meiosis.**

<u>Telophase</u>. Chromatids reach the poles, the nuclear envelope reforms, cytokinesis.

a. Move your chromosomes to the poles.

b. Redraw the nuclear envelope

c. Draw cytokinesis using your chalk

d. You should have 2 cells with two **homologous** chromosomes.

Model mitosis for your TA.

Observing Mitosis in Preserved Specimens

Materials
Prepared slide of onion root tip
Compound microscope

Procedure
Observe and **draw** all the stages of the cell cycle (Interphase, prophase, metaphase, anaphase and telophase) from the prepared slide of the onion root tip. (Rust p. 4, fig 4 a-e)

NOTES

Meiosis

Purpose
To gain an understanding of mitosis and meiosis using bead models and prepared slides.

Objectives
After completing this lab, you should be able to:
- Explain the steps of mitosis using the bead model.
- Be able to identify the stages of mitosis from microscope slides
- Explain the steps of meiosis using the bead model.

Introduction
The nuclei in cells of eukaryotic organisms contain **chromosomes** with clusters of **genes**, discrete units of hereditary information consisting of double-stranded deoxyribonucleic acid (DNA). When cells divide, chromosomes are duplicated and passed on to daughter cells. Multicellular organisms have **reproductive cells** (eggs and sperm) as well as **somatic (body) cells**.

In somatic cells, as well as unicellular organisms, the nucleus divides by **mitosis** into two daughter nuclei. Each daughter nucleus has the same number of chromosomes and the same genes as the parent cell. In **diploid (2n)** organisms, there are two copies of each chromosome, that is, the chromosomes exist as **homologous pairs.** In **haploid (1n)** cells, each chromosome is represented only once. For example, human cells contain 23 different chromosomes (1n = 23), so diploid human cells contain a total of 46 chromosomes (2n = 46) – 23 pairs of homologous chromosomes. Homologous chromosomes are similar in that they are the same size and contain the same genes, but they are not identical because each chromosome of a given pair may contain a different **allele** of the same gene. For example, chromosome one may carry the eye color gene, but one of the homologous pairs may carry the blue color allele and the other may carry the brown color allele. Blue and brown are different alleles of one gene, the gene for eye color. Incidentally, the individual in the example above would be **heterozygous** for the eye color gene, because s/he carries different alleles on each chromosome of the homologous chromosome one pair. If the above individual carried two identical eye color alleles, one on each of the homologues, s/he would be termed **homozygous** for the eye color gene. Since mitosis is a form of **clonal reproduction**, if the parent cell was diploid, the daughter cells will be diploid. It should be noted that if the parent cell were haploid, for example as in bacteria and fungi, the daughter cell will also be haploid.

In multicellular organisms, **meiosis** takes place in preparation for sexual reproduction. In contrast to mitosis, meiosis only takes place in diploid cells, and results in **four haploid** cells. These cells become the **gametes**--the egg and sperm cells--that produce the next generation. Another difference between meiosis and mitosis is that the homologous pairs may exchange sections of DNA with each other in the process of **recombination**. Thus, mitosis produces two genetically identical daughter cells, and meiosis produces four genetically different haploid daughter cells.

Modeling Meiosis with Beads

Meiosis with one pair of homologous chromosomes

Procedure

1. Make two chromosomes with beads. Each chromosome should be 14 beads long with a centromere in the middle. One of the chromosomes should be red and the other should be pink. This is your **homologous pair** of chromosomes.

2. Replicate your chromosomes as in mitosis. Occurs in "S" phase of the cell cycle.

Meiosis I

3. Prophase I -- this is the first stage of meiosis.

   a. Prophase begins when chromosomes begin to coil and condense.

   b. Nuclear envelope breaks down. Erase your chalk nuclear membrane.

   c. During prophase I, homologous chromosomes, each consisting of two sister chromatids, line up alongside each other. This process is known as **synapsis.** The group of paired, replicated, homologous chromosomes is called a **tetrad** (because it consists of four chromosomes). This is the stage at which recombination may take place. **This process does not occur in mitosis.**

   d. Spindles form. Draw a spindle with chalk on your bench, with a spindle fiber from each pole associated with the kinetochore of each pair of sister chromatids.

4. Metaphase I -- Replicated homologous chromosomes line up in the middle of the cell.

   a. Replicated pairs of homologous chromosomes are lined up alongside each other. **This is different from the manner the chromosomes lined up during metaphase of mitosis.**

5. Anaphase I -- Homologous pairs begin to separate and move towards the poles.

   a. Separate your homologous pair and move them to opposite poles. The sister chromatids remain attached. **The sister chromatids separate during anaphase of mitosis.**

6. Telophase I -- Sister chromatids reach the poles, cytokinesis takes place.

   a. Move your chromosomes to the poles.

   b. Draw cytokinesis using your chalk.

   c. You should have 2 cells with one pair of **replicated** chromosomes.

Meiosis II

7. Prophase II -- **Chromosomes do not replicate before starting meiosis II**

   a. Prophase begins when chromosomes begin to coil and condense.

   b. Spindles form. Draw a spindle with chalk on your bench, with a spindle fiber from each pole associated with the kinetochore of each pair of sister chromatids.

8. Metaphase II -- Replicated chromosomes line up in the middle of the cell.

   a. Your sister chromatids should be lined up in the middle of the cell **exactly as they were during metaphase of mitosis.**

9. <u>Anaphase II</u> -- Sister chromatids begin to separate and move towards the poles.

   a. Separate your sister chromatids **at the centromere** and begin moving them towards the opposite poles. (**This process is the same as for anaphase of mitosis**).

10. <u>Telophase II</u> -- Chromatids reach the poles, nuclear membrane reforms, cytokinesis takes place.

    a. Move your chromosomes to opposite poles.

    b. Redraw the nuclear membrane.

    c. Draw cytokinesis using your chalk

    d. You should have 4 cells with one chromosome each. These cells will become **gametes.**

The fact that *homologous* chromosomes *segregate* into different gametes is the basis of Mendel's **Law of Segregation.**

Meiosis with two pairs of homologous chromosomes

Procedure
1. Build another pair of homologues that are short (6 beads), one yellow and one green. You should have 4 chromosomes in your cell. Red and pink long and yellow and green short.

2. Repeat meiosis steps from above (#2-10).

3. At the end of meiosis, you should have 4 gametes with 2 **nonhomologous** chromosomes in each cell. Note which color beads are in which cell.

You may have discovered that the two pairs of homologous chromosomes in this exercise can line up in two different patterns:

Red : Pink   OR   Red : Pink
Blue : Green   Green : Blue

The fact that *nonhomologous* chromosomes sort themselves *independently* of each other is the basis of Mendel's **Law of Independent Assortment.** Use your two pairs of homologous chromosomes to model independent assortment an the appropriate step above.

Also, use your two pairs of homologous chromosomes to model **Recombination** (crossing over) between non-sister chromatids at the appropriate step above.

Model mitosis for your TA.

NOTES

Drosophila

Purpose
To gain an understanding of basic fruit fly (*Drosophila melanogaster*) experimental techniques
To learn to recognize a wild type fruit fly phenotype and to learn several mutant traits
To identify the mutant phenotypes segregating in your F2 progeny
To score the four phenotypic classes
To understand more about the inheritance of these genes

Objectives
After completing this lab, you should be able to:
- Score, transfer, and cross fruit flies without killing them
- Be able to identify key phenotypic characteristics of fruit flies
- Be able to identity several mutant traits (**phenotypic markers**)

Supporting material in textbook
Chapters 14 and 15 contain information about basic genetics. In particular, note Figures 14.8 (p. 276), 15.2 (p. 295, and 15.4 (p. 297), and 15.9 (p. 301).

Calendar
Week 1 (today):
   Basic fruit fly care and maintenance
   Learn to recognize wild type *Drosophila* & *vestigial* (*vg*), *ebony* (*e*), and *sepia* (*se*) mutations
   Make an F2 cross of your F1 unknown

Weeks 3 & 4:
   Determine the mutant genes present in your cross
   Score phenotypic classes by gender
   Determine phenotypic ratios

Introduction
Genetic terms: Gene, allele, phenotype, genotype, trait, wild type, mutant, segregation, independent assortment, F1, and F2.

Fly terms: egg, instar, larva, pupa, adult

Fruit flies (*Drosophila melanogaster*) have been a commonly used experimental organism since around 1900, when **Thomas Hunt Morgan** first began experimenting with them. Most of our understanding of basic genetics and chromosome behavior comes from studies with *Drosophila*. Concepts such as the **chromosomal basis of heredity**, **sex linkage** and **gene linkage** are a direct result of Morgan's work with fruit flies. In addition, the chromosomal basis of Mendel's "Laws" — **segregation** and **independent assortment** — was shown through research with *Drosophila*. Hence, understanding of how these experiments were performed is mandatory for a thorough understanding of basic genetic principles.

This laboratory occurs in three parts. In the first section, today's lab, you will learn the basic techniques of how to anesthetize fruit flies, sort them, and transfer them to new vials without killing them. You will also learn to recognize a wild type fruit fly, and you will learn to recognize fruit flies harboring mutations in specific genes (which demonstrate altered traits or phenotypic

31

markers). In two weeks, you will receive a vial of **unknown F1 flies**. These flies are the progeny of a cross between two fruit fly lines, each carrying a mutation in a different gene. You will make an **F2 cross** by mating male and female F1 flies. Hence, in this experiment you will be following the inheritance of two different genes. In four weeks, you will score the **F2 progeny** to determine if, and how, the two genes are related to each other.

Know your Organism

Your experiment will run more smoothly, and have a higher likelihood of success, if you familiarize yourself with the fruit fly life cycle. *Drosophila melanogaster* is in the insect order Diptera. The Dipterans all have **complete metamorphosis**. This means there are four distinct stages: egg, three larval stages (called **instars**), pupal, and adult. The *Drosophila* lifecycle is complete in about two weeks: ~one week in the egg and larval stages and ~one week in the pupa. The egg and 1st instar larval stages are difficult to see without a microscope. The 3rd instar larvae will climb up the side of the vial and form a pupal case. Adult flies hatch from the pupal cases.

Notation

Genetic notation is not universal for all experimental organisms. It is imperative you become comfortable with at least two types—that used by Mendel and that devised by Morgan for fruit flies. A table comparing them is provided below.

	Mendel	**Morgan**
Wild type[1]	R—round seed G—green seed P—purple flower	e^+—normal body (carmel) se^+—normal eye (red) vg^+—normal wing (flat)
Mutant[2]	r—wrinkled seed g—yellow seed p—white flower	e—ebony body se—sepia eye vg—vestigial (wrinkled) wings
Homozygote[3]	RR or rr	e^+/e^+ or se^+/se^+
Heterozygote	Rr or Gg	e^+/e or se^+/se
Dihybrid[4]	RrGg	vg^+/vg ; e^+/e
Gamete for two genes	RG, Rg, or rg	$e^+ vg^+$, $e^+ vg$, or $e\ vg$

[1] and [2]—"wild type" is not a term used by Mendel. He identified variants and denoted the dominant allele of a gene with an uppercase letter. Morgan's notation recognizes organisms have a "normal" phenotype (wild type) and a variation from this phenotype represents a mutant. Thus, the wild type allele always carries a + superscript. The gene is named for the <u>mutant</u> phenotype. For example, *se* represents the *sepia* gene, which, when normal, causes red eyes (se^+) in flies, but when mutant (se) causes sepia (brownish) eyes. Most mutations (**and all the ones used in this lab**) are **recessive**, denoted by lower case letters as with Mendel. A dominant mutation would utilize an uppercase letter. Hence, B^+—normal eyes, B—bar eyes, and B is dominant to B^+.

[3] and [4]—Your textbook uses $se^+ se^+$ omitting the /. This can be confusing when dealing with a dihybrid. In lecture and in lab we always will use a / to denote *different alleles of a gene*, and a semicolon (;) to denote *different genes* (e.g. e^+/e ; vg^+/vg)

WEEK 1

You will observe the fly stocks listed below. We will demonstrate the relevant features of wild type fruit flies, how to tell males and females apart, and how to identify the mutant phenotypes. **However, remember that you will not know the identity of the mutant genes present in your F1 stock. Hence, you must take good notes in today's lab, so that you are able to correctly identify the phenotypes of the mutants when they appear in your F2 progeny.**

Stock	Phenotype
wild type	Carmel colored body, crimson red eyes, full wings.
vg (*vestigial*)	Wrinkly, stunted wings. They can't fly but they sure can jump.
se (*sepia*)	Brownish eyes, facets are less obvious than wild type.
e (*ebony*)	Dark body. Compare with a wild type fly if ambiguous.

To observe the flies more easily, you must get them to stop moving. We do this by anesthetizing them with carbon dioxide. Carbon dioxide is injected briefly and carefully into an inverted tube containing flies until all the flies are "knocked out". The flies then are emptied onto a special carbon dioxide pad, keeping them asleep for scoring. It is important to keep the flies out of the food during this process. They can get stuck and die.

Once the flies are safely on the carbon dioxide pad, arrange them in a neat, straight line with a paintbrush. Observe the flies to learn wild type and mutant phenotypes. Use a paintbrush or probe to manipulate the flies. A brush works well for moving the flies but is not good for manipulating fly structures such as wings and legs. Use a probe for this, taking care not to puncture the abdomen and killing the fly.

When you are done observing a stock, push the flies into a pile with a paintbrush and then carefully push the pile back into the tube. Try to avoid letting the flies fall onto the food. Leave the vial on its side until the flies have woken up (only a few minutes).

Before receiving your F1 stock vial, you first must pass the *Drosophila* Scoring Quiz. See your TA for details.

Making a Cross

1. Obtain an **unknown F1** stock vial from Ken or your TA. These flies are the offspring of a cross between two mutant lines.

2. Anesthetize and manipulate the flies as described above. All should look wild type because **both mutations are recessive.** Thus, the genotype of these F1 flies is $m1^+/m1; m2^+/m2$, where "m" stands for "mutant." These are the parents of the F2 generation you will score in two weeks. **Remember, if all goes well, you will discard these F1's before next lab.**

3. Sort the F1s by gender (2 lines). Count each and report the totals to Ken. He will advise you how many flies of each gender you should place into each of your labeled vials.

4. Carefully place the prescribed numbers of flies into each vial as it lay on its side. Keep the flies out of the food, but push them far enough in so they aren't crushed by the stopper

WEEKS 3 & 4

You will finish the *Drosophila* experiment you began two weeks ago by scoring (counting) the F2 progeny of your cross. You may need to come in to lab several times to gather enough data to complete this laboratory. Come in for a few minutes every day to score progeny. Follow the steps below to collect and analyze your data.

1. Determine the **mutant genes** present in your unknown, based upon notes you took week 1

2. Determine how many **phenotypic classes** are present in your F2 progeny

3. Count the number of flies in each phenotypic class by gender

4. Determine the **phenotypic ratio** of each class. (# of flies in a class / total # of flies scored)

Scoring Mutant Traits
1. Anesthetize flies as before. *Push them into a nice, straight line* with a paintbrush. This makes it much easier to observe each fly individually, and to count phenotypic classes.

2. Use your probe to analyze eye color, body color, and the wings. Remember, you will have some combination of **two** mutants (*vg*, *e*, and *se*). Thus, you need to observe your F2 flies to determine if some have a wing mutation (*vg*), if the eyes are not wild type (*se*), or if the body is darker than wild type (*e*). Use your notes from Week 1. Another useful trick is to anesthetize a few wild type flies, males and females, for comparison. This is particularly helpful with *se* and *e*.

3. There are many ways to count flies; it's really not that complicated. Your primary goal is **accuracy**, so whatever system you come up with to achieve this goal is great. Here's how I do it. Let's say I'm observing my F2 progeny and I notice, in addition to many wild type flies, some have truncated wings. I figure that *vg* is segregating in my F2 population. I also notice some seem considerably darker than others, so I figure I also have *e* segregating. I now have determined three phenotypic classes: wild type, *e*, and *vg*. I know, being a clever geneticist, I also should see a fourth class with both mutations present, i.e., *vg ; e*. So now I go through my line of flies from **# 1 above** and I push all the *vg* flies out of the line. I carefully observe them to see if they are <u>also</u> *e*. Let's say there are 8 *vg* flies that have a wild type body color, i.e., they are *vg ; e⁺*. I find 2 flies that seem to be <u>both</u> *vg* and *e*, i.e., they are *vg ; e*. I now go back to the line and count all the flies that are *e* (*vg⁺*; *b*), verifying whether or not they are <u>also</u> *vg*. Lastly, I count all the wild type flies.

❖ **Check your F2s every day** and score vials as necessary. This means you don't have to score too many flies at once and data isn't lost because of overcrowding issues.

❖ **Tabulate your data as you collect it and keep running totals of the F2 phenotypes scored.** This will provide you with the information needed to answer the inevitable question:

❖ **"When can I quit counting flies?"** There is no standard answer to this question. In genetics, the more data, the better. So, the best answer to this question is: "When your data are clear enough for definitive interpretation." This depends on many factors, but if you tabulate your data daily, we should be able to tell you when you have enough data.

Questions for Understanding

1. What are the two mutations present in your **unknown**?

2. List the four **phenotypic classes** you scored in your F2 progeny and indicate the number flies in each class.

3. State the **phenotypic ratios** observed in your F2 progeny.

4. Are the genes you studied located on **sex chromosomes** or **autosomes**? How do you know?

5. Are your two genes **independently assorting** or are they **linked**? How do you know?

6. Are these two genes located on the **same chromosome** or on **different chromosomes**? How do you know, and can you be sure?

NOTES